Letters *from* Heaven

An Illuminated Alphabet

by Susan Kelly vonMedicus

with
poems by Ginny Eliason Silva

Conciliar Press
Ben Lomond, California

Letters From Heaven: An Illuminated Alphabet

Illuminations, introduction, references, prayers, and symbol quest page,
© copyright 2000 by Susan Kelly vonMedicus

Poems © copyright 2000 by Ginny Eliason Silva

First printed 2000.
Reprinted 2001.

Published by   Conciliar Press
              P.O. Box 76
              Ben Lomond, California 95005-0076

Printed in Hong Kong

ISBN 1-888212-18-7

Library of Congress Cataloging-in-Publication Data

Von Medicus, Susan Kelly, 1956-
    Letters from heaven : an illuminated alphabet / by Susan Kelly
von Medicus ; with poems by Ginny Eliason Silva.
    p. cm.
ISBN 1-888212-18-7
    1. Bible stories.   [1. Bible stories. 2. Alphabet.]   I. Silva,
Ginny Eliason, 1957-   II. Title.
    BS551.2 .V64 2000
    220.9'505--dc21
                                                 00-031773

ACKNOWLEDGMENTS AND DEDICATIONS

I began this alphabet book of saints and mysteries eight years ago with illuminations for each letter and accompanying text and prayers. I am delighted with Ginny Silva's poems, which wonderfully maintain my intent to present imagery as more than allegory, as symbolic and transcendent. Thank you for this excellent work, Ginny. I thank my children for their patience with a long overdue Christmas gift, my sister-in-law Karen for her advice and humor, and my husband for his constant support of all my endeavors.   —S. vM.

*As it started, a gift for my children—William, Brenden, and Freeman—
and offered to the glory of the Most Holy Trinity.*

Susan, I was overcome by your beautiful artwork from the moment I saw it—truly, your paintings illumine my path. Jeff, thanks for your encouragement, guidance, and unfailing good cheer—on these I depended, as always.   —G. S.

For Hank, Tommy, Joey, Jamie, Grace, Susanna, and Maria.

Introduction

The illuminated letters in this alphabet are Irish Uncial Majuscule, an ancient script which was developed during the sixth to ninth centuries. When St. Patrick was a boy in England, he was captured by pirates and taken as a slave to Ireland. He escaped to France, and eventually became a bishop. He decided to return to Ireland, and so became the first to bring the good news of Christ to the Irish. He also brought with him Latin prayer books handwritten in Roman Uncial lettering. The Irish monks contributed their own unique qualities to the script, and over time it became the distinctive Irish Uncial.

The illustrations are done in the medieval manner using gold leaf on red clay and egg tempera color work. The imagery combines traditional saints, narrative, and symbols of the Eastern Orthodox, Roman, and Anglican Catholic faiths.

ngel of
god

Angel of God

Angels bring messages from heaven to earth—
Once to the shepherds they told of Christ's birth.
Their choirs in heaven still sing of His glory
Proclaiming the Lord of the Sabbath is holy.
Faster than lightning, more luminous than stars,
Their obedience is wisdom, it brightens the dark.
God in His love gave an angel of light
To watch over you every day and all night.
Pray to your angel to guard you from sin,
To keep your heart open so Love will come in.

Genesis 28: 12

Angel of God, take my prayers to God.
Let me know His power and light.

Brendan, Saint and Navigator

This monk lived in Ireland in the sixth century;
With Christ for his anchor, he traveled the seas.
In a small leather boat over cold northern waves
He sailed past the known world—Oh he was brave!
The ocean held islands of puffins and sheep,
Fields of stars in the night sky, storms in the deep.
Long before Columbus, to America he came—
Because he trusted in God, we honor his name.

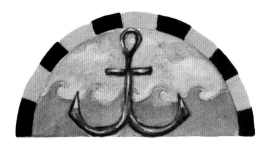

Feast Day: May 16

Saint Brendan,
come to my aid when I feel lost at sea.

Brendan saint and navigator

Cherubim, Guardians to the Tree of Life

In a beautiful garden in Paradise
Runs an ancient clear river, the water of life.
There the cherubim surround a majestic tree
Whose twelve kinds of fruit are for you and for me.
With fiery swords turning every direction
These angels show us God's constant protection.
To the Tree of Life they are guarding the way
So that those who love God may enter one day.

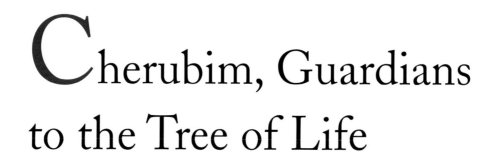

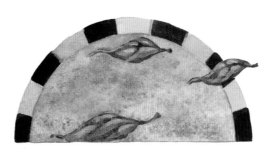

Genesis 3:24

O mighty cherubim,
bring me close to God.

Cherubim guardian to the tree of life

DAVID, KING
PROPHET
AND SINGER OF
PSALMS

TRULY my soul waiteth upon God. from him cometh my salvation ☀

Psalms 62:1

David:
King, Prophet,
and Singer of Psalms

In the Bethlehem hills, land of olives and palms

Lived Jesse's son David, not yet king at all,

But only a harp-playing shepherd, so small

Who wrote hymns of praise to the great King of All.

When the Philistines came (they were giants, and strong),

The army of Israel couldn't last long.

Unafraid, David chose five stones from the riverbed;

Grown men were trembling, but soon Goliath lay dead.

Soldier, musician, and leader of men,

Prophet whose psalms will be known to the end.

The Book of Psalms

Holy David,
inspire me to sing a joyful song of praise to the Lord.

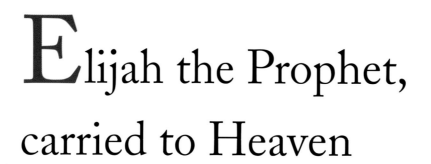

Elijah the Prophet, carried to Heaven

Oh sing of Elijah, the prophet of old
Whom Ahab and Jezebel considered too bold.
The prophets of Baal were put to great shame
When in spite of their howls, Elijah's prayers brought a flame.
He fled to the wilderness and lived by dry streams,
Protected by angels, enlightened by dreams,
Fed by a raven, who brought him his bread—
At the time of his death, he went by chariot instead.

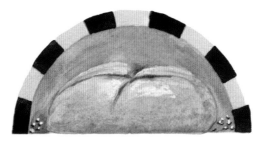

Second Kings 2

Thanks be to God!
You give us the bread of life!

Elijah the prophet carried to heaven

FORERUNNER SAINT JOHN THE BAPTIST

Forerunner, Saint John the Baptist

As a babe in the womb when Mary came to his mother,
John leaped with joy at the approach of his Savior.
Sent to bear witness to the light of the Son,
John fasted and prayed in the desert alone.
Eating locusts and honey, and dressed in rough skins
He announced, "the Kingdom of God now begins."
Angel of the wilderness, to Israel he called,
Telling people to make their hearts ready for God.
He baptized the repentant in the Jordan River—
Saying Jesus would baptize not with water, but fire.
John baptized his Cousin in humility and love,
Saw the Spirit descend in the form of a dove.

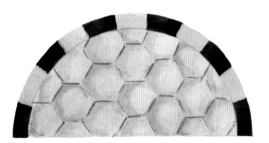

Luke 3:15–18

Saint John, angel of the wilderness,
help me to do God's work.

George, Saint and Dragon-Slayer

George was a commander in the old times of Rome
Who was taught to love Christ in his childhood home.
The emperor's trophy-bearer, handsome and strong,
A young man of twenty who knew right from wrong.
When Diocletian gave orders to worship false gods
George told him his duty was to make good and fair laws.
The spears of the soldiers against George were waged
By this ruler of empires who was ruled by his rage.
Through trials and tortures, George calmly endured
Till the dragon of evil's defeat was secured.

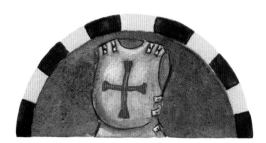

Feast Day: April 23

O brave Saint George,
protect those less fortunate.

eorse
saint and
drason
slaser

Holy Anna, Mother of Mary

The wife without child, growing tired and old
Instead of despairing, in her prayers became bold.
"Even the earth brings forth fruit, why is it
That we alone of Israel You have not chosen to visit?"
Her husband Joachim, a righteous man of the herds,
Of what he received always gave away two-thirds.
He pleaded with God when he could no longer bear
The shame of their barrenness, "Lord, give us an heir!"
Gabriel appeared to them, from heaven he flew;
Beyond all hope, their hope would come true.
He told them they would to a daughter give birth,
A daughter whose Child would be God come to earth.

Feast Day: July 26

Saint Anna,
help me believe God's promises.

Hols Anna mother of mars

Ic xc:
Jesus Christ

There are times when an abbreviation is better
So that people read quickly, with only one look.
To make them the Greeks took the first and last letter
Of the word they were using in icons or books.
Since IHCOUC was Jesus, they spelled IC for that,
And XPICTOC for Christ became XC—like that.
Alpha and Omega, beginning and end,
Christ was before all and through all, mankind's only friend.

Matthew 1:23

Jesus Christ, have mercy on me,
now and always.

ohn the divine saint and revealer

John the Divine, Saint and Revealer

John was the apostle the Lord loved as a brother,
Whom He told from the Cross, "Behold, your mother."
John was the young one, who was not even twenty
Though of wisdom and love, he had been graced with plenty.
He was there on Mt. Tabor with Christ in His glory;
After labors and trials he wrote down the story
Of the good news of Christ, and asked us to love,
Saying by this men would know the one God above.
John was banished to Patmos, and there had a vision—
He wrote what God told him in the book Revelation.

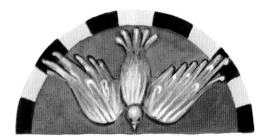

Revelation 22:16–21

May the peace of the Lord
be with us all.

Katherine, saint and martyr

Katherine, Saint and Martyr

A beautiful princess, a scholar while young,
Katherine of Egypt was skilled with her tongue.
Debating philosophers from near and from far,
She sought after Truth, and He came to her
In a vision of Mary and her Savior, her Son.
She scorned the knowledge she had eagerly won
As nothing to the Light of the wisdom Christ gave
And began to teach others of this One who could save.
The father she loved turned her in to the governor
But do what he would, he could not even frighten her.
The councillors, the scholars, and even his wife
Were convinced by her speeches that Christ brings us life.
Miracles followed each trial she went through;
Now this holy martyr is praying for you.

Feast Day: November 25

Show me, Saint Katherine,
how to learn all I can about my faith.

Lamb of God Christ our Lord

Lamb of God, Christ our Lord

Good Shepherd of God, who loves all of His flock,
Who waits for the door of our hearts to unlock,
Who leaves ninety-nine to search after the one
And listens for the steps of each prodigal son,
Was also, the day when the sun turned dark,
The Lamb of God on whom men left their mark.
The Lamb slain for Isaac, for all time, for the world,
On the Cross Christ's banner of love was unfurled.

John 1:29

Dear Christ, find me when I am lost,
and gently bring me back to your flock.

Michael, Leader of the Archangels

Leader of archangels, brave and strong,
Be with us and help us to fight against wrong.
Victorious over Lucifer, you drove him from Heaven,
Help us now as we try to resist Satan's leaven.
You who spoke to Moses from the bush that burned,
Speak to us, remind us to do as we've learned.
You kept Abraham's knife from its deathly art;
From the wounds of the evil one, defend our hearts.

Genesis 22:10–14

Saint Michael, great victor over Satan,
protect me from all evil.

Michael Leader of Archangels

Nicholas, Saint and Wonderworker

Nicholas was a bishop who loved young and old
And the poor, whom he helped every day of the year.
To three helpless daughters he tossed sacks of gold
To redeem them from lives of slavery and fear.
As a young man in Myra he inherited great wealth
But he gave it all up, keeping none for himself.
In the whole of Lycia he was known and revered;
His wisdom, his courage, and his mercy were clear.
In persecutions he suffered, in the First Council prevailed—
From those days till now, his prayers have not failed.

Feast Day: December 6

O holy Saint Nicholas,
teach me generosity.

Nicholas, saint and
wonderworker

Obadiah holy prophet

and the king-dom shall be the Lords
Ob.1.21

Obadiah, Holy Prophet

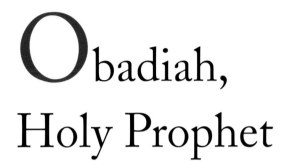

Nine hundred years before Christ, Obadiah served
In the court of King Ahab, never losing his nerve.
Not bowing to idols, he worshipped only the Lord.
When Jezebel's army took up their swords
To hunt down the prophets, Obadiah was brave—
He sheltered a hundred of them in a cave.
Follower of Elijah, and like him in ways
He loved God and served Him to the end of his days.

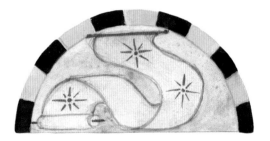

The Book of Obadiah

Dear Lord, keep me like Obadiah,
unselfish and unafraid to proclaim Your goodness.

Peter and Paul, Holy Apostles of our Lord

Leaders of Apostles, rock and scribe of the Church,
They gave strength and wisdom to all who would search.
Peter was called from his fishing nets to come,
The first to confess where Jesus was from.
Peter walked on the water, across the high waves,
Saul walked to Damascus and by God's light was saved.
From persecutor of Christ to proclaimer of Truth,
Paul was a bearer of spiritual fruit.

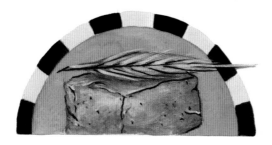

Matthew 16:18, 19 • Acts 9:1–22

Saints Peter and Paul, great leaders of our Church,
give me strength and conviction.

Peter and Paul, holy apostles of our Lord

Queen of
heaven
mother of
christ

Queen of Heaven, Mother of Christ

Attired in righteousness, Mother of Love
Who united the realms below and above,
Your veil and your cloak are the color of clay,
One of us, of the earth, you taught us to pray.
Your robe is of heaven, blue like the sky—
Heaven in your womb is the reason why.
You were the meeting place of heaven and earth
From the hour Gabriel told you the plan for Christ's birth.
As handmaid of the Lord on earth you were seen—
In heaven, still serving, you are our Queen.

Luke 1:46–56

Holy Mary, bring my prayers to your beloved Son
who holds you so close.

Rafael, Archangel of Light

Of seven archangels, Rafael is one;

He heals with God's light and shines like the sun.

He taught Tobias to use parts of a fish

To help his blind father see the world as he wished.

Other parts he used to put demons to flight

So Tobias and his bride could live a long life.

To Noah he brought God's exact instructions

For gopherwood and pitch in the Ark's construction.

For work on the earth, he has two feathery wings,

And two wings of light when in heaven he sings.

Tobit 2:1–12

Bring God's healing power to everyone,
O splendid Archangel Rafael.

Star of Bethlehem, leading us to Christ

The Magi were Gentiles, astrologers from afar
Who followed a star seeking the Maker of stars.
The light seen from the East meant a King of true worth;
When they found Him the wise kings rejoiced in His birth.
The Savior's location they would not betray—
Too clever for Herod, they went home a new way.
Their gifts were symbolic; the gold for God's might,
The frankincense for offering prayers as is right,
And myrrh for His suffering, anointing oil for the dead.
God blessed them by sending His star overhead.

Matthew 2:1–12

God, my heavenly Father,
guide me as I walk gazing at the stars.

Thomas, Saint and Believer

After the Cross, when Jesus rose before dawn,
He came to the disciples, but Thomas was gone.
Thomas, not believing the news that he heard,
Had to see with his own eyes, he could not take their word.
So Christ came again, knowing even strong men are frail
And asked Thomas to touch the prints of the nails.
He felt the Lord's side, found the sword's ruthless mark—
"My Lord and my God" was the cry from his heart.
At that time, and all time that has since come to be,
His doubts have shown Christ to those longing to see.

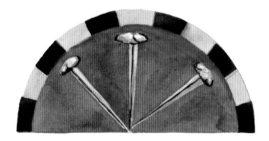

John 20:24–29

Saint Thomas,
strengthen my faith in the mysteries of God.

Thomas, saint and believer

Uriel, Archangel

One angel has the fire of God from above,

A fire that burns with the fierce flame of Love.

He wrestled with Jacob by the river all night,

Jacob's limp from the hip was the mark of the fight.

Uriel warned Noah of the Flood soon to come

So he would know why and when, and where it came from.

To the dark gates of Hades he keeps safe the key

So that those who love God will all be set free.

Genesis 32:24–30

Glorious Archangel Uriel,
help me hear God's voice.

Virgin of Tenderness

The young girl of tenderness, who kept all in her heart,
Whose purity and love always set her apart,
Wrapped Jesus in swaddling clothes and nursed Him with love,
Knowing her Child was her Lord from above.
She sheltered the God/man, just a wee baby boy
And sensed that His life the world would try to destroy.
Bless the Rose without thorns, who loves great and small,
Who gave birth to Christ and became mother of us all.

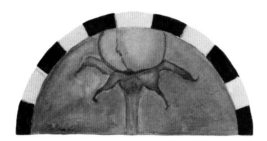

Luke 2:16–20

O blessed Mother Mary,
may your love embrace me.

Virgin of
tenoer-
ness

Women at
the Tomb

Women at the Tomb

Mary Mother of God, Mary Magdalene, Joanna,
Salome, the sisters of Lazarus, and Susanna,
Rose early and hastened to the tomb of the Lord
With spices and oils for the Crucified One.
An earthquake, an angel, the great stone rolled aside—
The soldiers guarding the dead fell down like they'd died.
With clothing like snow and a face bright as lightning
The angel spoke kindly, knowing all this was frightening:
"Why seek ye the living among the dead?
Go tell the disciples He is risen, as He said."
They ran from the tomb with fear and great gladness
To tell of Christ's Resurrection, the end of all sadness.

Matthew 28: 1–10

*Heavenly Father, we approach you with thanksgiving
for the gift of eternal life.*

Xenia Saint and Fool for Christ

Xenia, Saint and Fool for Christ

A widow in Russia, the captain's young wife—
Xenia, when he died, began a new life.
Her husband's coat on her back, and old boots on her feet,
She weathered the cold in St. Petersburg streets.
She gave her belongings away, and even her home,
And for forty-five years as an outcast she roamed.
When given alms she fed those who had none;
In poverty a rich life in God had begun.
It was love for God, not the madness of men
That made her look like a fool to her friends.

Feast Day: January 24

*May your pure love of God and devotion to a simple life
inspire me, Saint Xenia.*

Young Jesus teaching

The Passover feast, then the caravan home—
When Joseph and Mary knew You were gone
They returned to Jerusalem, hurrying fast.
After three days they found You in the Temple at last,
As a boy, in humility asking questions of men,
In Your divinity with answers astounding them.
To Your earthly parents You gave a gentle reminder
Of obedience to the will of Your natural Father.
Without anger or offense You spoke to Your own
And with love went back with them to Your home.

Luke 2:41–52

Holy Family,
let me take your loving example to my family.

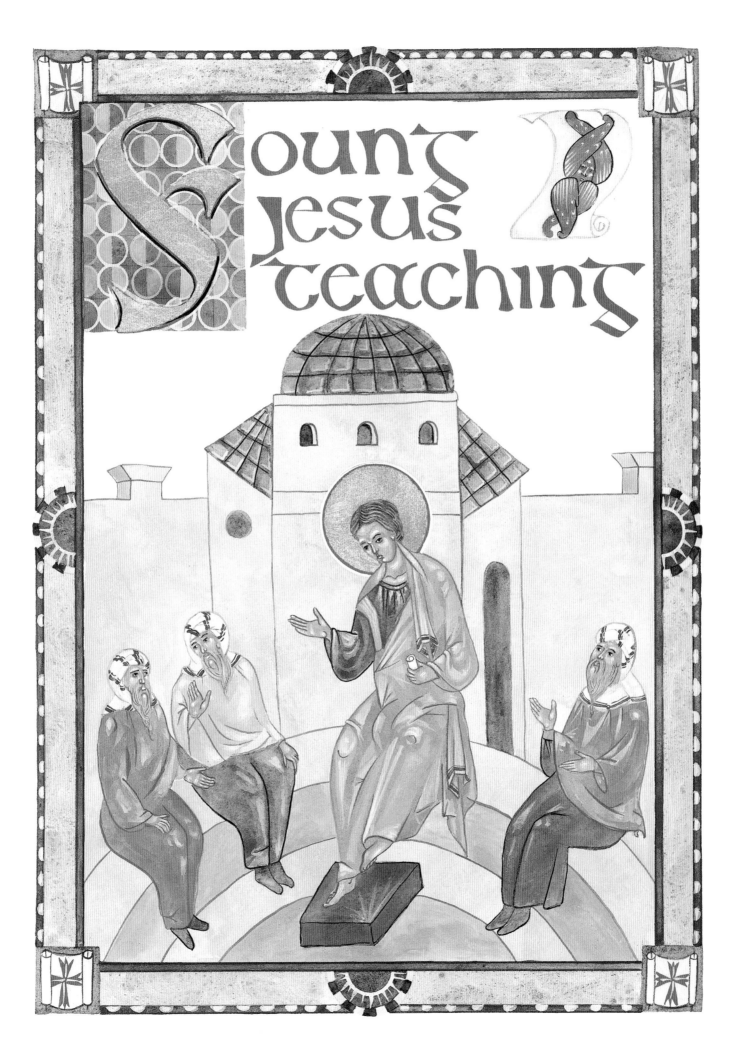

Mount Jesus teaching

Zachariah, Father of the Forerunner

High priest of the Temple, Zachariah was there
To lead three-year-old Mary up the long marble stairs.
His wife was Elizabeth; they were both old and sad
Thinking of the children they might have had.
One day while offering incense at the altar
He saw a glorious light that made his heart falter—
An angel, who told him to name his child John.
Unbelieving, he asked how could they have a son?
Nine months of silence, his boy's name on a slate;
Ever after his voice rose to heaven in praise.

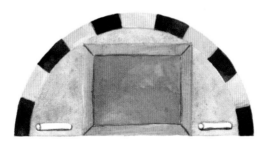

Luke 1:5–23

*Holy Zachariah, let me sing to the Lord
in my heart and with my lips.*

Symbol Quest

Look within these pages and you will see
many everyday things that are traditional Christian symbols.
Below are their meanings. Can you find them all?

	symbol	*meaning*
1	alpha and omega	the beginning and the end
2	anchor	hope
3	ark	a sacred vessel
4	armor	protection from evil
5	books	knowledge
6	bread	sustenance
7	chalk and slate	declaration
8	dove	peace
9	fire	the presence of the Holy Spirit
10	frankincense	to carry prayers on high
11	gold	Divine Light
12	honeybees	diligence
13	leaves	renewal
14	lilies	purity
15	lightning	enlightenment
16	music	praise
17	myrrh	suffering
18	nails	the Passion
19	oil	consecration
20	palm	victory
21	pen	teaching
22	rainbow	God's promise
23	rock	strength
24	rosary	devotion
25	rose without thorns	Mary, the Mother of God
26	scrolls	prophecy
27	shepherd's crook	authority
28	tools	obedience

Answer key:

a b c d

e f g h

i j k l

m n o p

q r s t

u v w x

y z